YOUR KNOWLEDGE HAS VALUE

Bibliographic information published by the German National Library:

The German National Library lists this publication in the National Bibliography; detailed bibliographic data are available on the Internet at http://dnb.dnb.de .

Imprint:

Copyright © 2018 GRIN Verlag
Print and binding: Books on Demand GmbH, Norderstedt Germany
ISBN: 9783346066091

This book at GRIN:

https://www.grin.com/document/505849

Moniruzzaman Kiron

Company Background and SWOT Analysis of Forever 21

GRIN Verlag

GRIN - Your knowledge has value

Since its foundation in 1998, GRIN has specialized in publishing academic texts by students, college teachers and other academics as e-book and printed book. The website www.grin.com is an ideal platform for presenting term papers, final papers, scientific essays, dissertations and specialist books.

Visit us on the internet:

http://www.grin.com/

http://www.facebook.com/grincom

http://www.twitter.com/grin_com

Table of Contents

1. Company Background

FOREVER 21 is known as one of the leading and most competitive fast fashion retail brands in the world. It is an American fashion retailer organization with the headquartered in **Los Angeles, California, USA** (MartinRoll, 2018). In **1984**, one immigrant couple from **South Korea *"Mr. Do Won Chang** and **Ms. Jin Sook Chang"*** have established the FOREVER 21 and named by their adorable daughter *"Tiev Forever"* whereas Mr. Do Won Chang occupying the post of CEO of the company. At the very beginning, it was known as ***"XX1 FOREVER"*** (FOREVER 21 Official Website, 2018). Forever 21 is competing on merchandise, cheap price points, prime locations, and rapid global logistics. According to Forbes, FOREVER 21 becomes the 5th largest American privet fast fashion retailer organization in 2018 (Forbes.com, 2018). Over the past 30 years, it has achieved some remarkable endeavors including the revenue of **USD8 billion** at the end of 2017. It has approximately 30,000 employees working in 790 retailer outlets of 48 nations. As it is a fashion retailer company so their main product is basically clothing, accessories and more than 60% of their clothes is made in China. Therefore, FOREVER 21 is capable of offering goods at a very cheap price towards its customers. The purpose of Forever 21 brand to compete directly with iconic global fashion brands like Zara, H&M, Uniqlo and some other key industry players (MartinRoll, 2018).

2. SWOT Analysis

SWOT analysis is considered as a useful method of understanding the Strengths, Weaknesses, Opportunities and Threats that involved with the organization. SWOT is use to identify the internal depth of the organization. SWOT is a method used to see the organizations' competitive position within the industry by assessing the possible standards for instance strengths and weakness. Moreover, SWOT helps the organization to establish and undertake strategies and activities more efficiently (GÜREL, 2018).

While the organization is willing to conduct the SWOT analysis, the organization must be realistic and probable upon sketch the strengths and weaknesses of the organization. However, the organization also need to be conscious of both positive and negative impacts. The dimensions of the SWOT are discoursed below:

2.1 Strengths

Strength is considered the very first feature of the SWOT analysis. Strength refers the favorable aspects or power of the organization. Moreover, strength reflects the internal perspective of the business and the customer's point of view. Organizational strengths can be financial position, brand image, high-tech structure, expert employee, product or service quality and etc. (GÜREL, 2017). For instance, Apple's strengths are its brand image, iPhone quality, financial position and such.

2.2 Weaknesses

Weaknesses refer the adverse aspects that take the organization away from its strengths. This are the aspects or factors shackled a firm from execution at its most favorable level. Lighting up the precise weaknesses supports a firm to recognize and overwhelm the lack of enthusiasm. A firm can loss its potential and productivity due to the weaknesses and initially end up with losing revenue. Weaknesses of an organization can be internal situation similar to insufficient resources, lack of capability, shortage of technology etc. (GÜREL, 2017).

2.3 Opportunities

This element of SWOT analysis tool analysis the external potential or prospectus of the organization in future arrangement execution. The variables drawn are consequence of current market and income reboots, capacity of business activity and increasing the value of items, underlining on market needs and so on. Opportunity assessment opens door for organizations to design and execute strategies to maximize the profitability (GÜREL, 2017). For example, fashion retailers can produce the garment products to the new market and increase the sales volume and market share.

2.4 Threats

Usually threats refer the unpleasant factors that can be risky for the organization. Threats are the characteristics that may have negative impacts on the organizations. Threats can be generated from the internal factors such as weaknesses and also can be from the external factors such as rivalry.

For example, inflation, new policy of government, new entrance in market, high volume of competition and such (GÜREL, 2017).

To conclude, SWOT analysis is a very effective tool to identify the potential and weaknesses of the company and also the tool open the doors for the company to find out the opportunities and identify the threats that can be harmful the company.

3. SWOT Analysis of Forever 21

Here, using SWOT as a guide we will be looking for the Strengths, Weaknesses, Opportunities and Threats of the Forever 21.

Strengths	Weaknesses	Opportunities	Threats
• **Latest trend.** • **Affordable.** • **Customer Savvy.**	• Private Organization. • Centralized. • Narrow Customer segmentation.	• Increasing Needs of Youngsters to Stick to Trends. • Customize Clothing.	• Very competitive market. • Fake imitations.

Figure: SWOT Analysis of Forever 21

3.1 Strengths of Forever 21

As a establish company Forever 21 has some unique strengths to differentiate itself from its rivals. The strengths are following below;

3.1.1. Latest Trends

One of the durable strengths of Forever 21 is it assumes the latest trends very quickly. Forever 21 has managed to place itself as a retailer that stays on trend at all times and has the hottest styles for its customers in all categories. Besides, the dresses are superior in quality, sophisticated, and designs are also very amazing (MARSH, 2018).

3.1.2 Affordable

People who love shopping will probably list down "Forever 21" on top their list because of the affordability. Forever 21 is fashion brand who retails cloths which is cheaper in price than its close competitors. Because of low-cost production and suppliers, they can manufacture low-cost goods

4

to their customers which provides Forever 21 to take the competitive advantage of the market. Although, Forever 21 is focused on offering low-cost cloths in the market but they are also aware of their product quality (Persad, 2015).

3.1.3 Customer Savvy

According to the report of The Guardian; Forever 21 is one of the most famous and customer-friendly fashion brands among the European region because of the magnificent designs. Most of the designs of Forever 21 come from its customers. Moreover, to confirming that feedback from the customers are transformed into reality, Forever 21 has a very storing system of recording of the voice of the customers. Therefore, Forever 21 does not focus at the high end and expends but emphases more on receiving opinion, suggestions and comments from its customers and executing it at the initial outcomes (Wiseman, 2011).

3.2 Weaknesses of Forever 21

Even though Forever 21 has positioned themselves one of the well-known fashion brands yet it has some weaknesses which can be harsh for the company. The weaknesses include;

3.2.1 Private Organization

Even though Forever 21 is a fast fashion retailer who obtain the outlets all over the world with a predictable assets of $4.1bilion yet, the company is still carry on and likely to be a family owned business. Because of the fact the company own a poor market share and the growth of the company is not visible. On the other hand, the financial structure of the company is very weak compare to its rivals due to restricted assets on capital market (Batheja, 2018).

3.2.2 Centralized

As Forever 21 is being recognized as a family owned business therefore lots of the organizational and operational as well as the decision making process comes from the owner which set apart the company is not too welcome to consider the proposals from other stakeholders. (Gomes, 2006)

3.2.3 Narrow Customer Segmentation

'Forever 21' has only been focused on a certain segmentation of the market right from the beginning of the company. The company is recognized as a fashion brand for the young adults.

The over connotation with teenagers and young adults has formed a hesitation or unwillingness amongst the adult customers to purchase clothes from Forever 21. Therefore, sooner or later it may convert as a hazard for Forever 21 (Lutz, 2013).

3.3 Opportunities for Forever 21

Opportunities bring up to those possibilities in the market for Forever 21 which the company can take advantage of increasing the revenues. The opportunities include;

3.3.1 Increasing Needs of Youngsters to Stick to Trends

In this century probably fashion is changing most quickly. In other words, which is updated today probably backdated tomorrow. The young generation are not only focused on trends but also tentative to dress properly. As Forever 21 is a fast fashion brand this is a huge opportunity for them to capitalize the norms of stick to the trend (Wiseman, 2011).

3.3.2 Customized Clothing

Nowadays most of the individuals favor to buy the clothes that they fill comfortable of wearing. Particularly in order to make sure that they look different from the crowd; the high-end people always exercise something personalized or customized. This tendency of people has become a very general strategy to brand customize attire. This is a great opportunity for the Forever 21 to customize the clothing so that customers stick with them.

3.4 Threats of Forever 21

Threats are the issues in the surroundings that can be harmful for the company to grow in the market. Threats include;

3.4.1 Very competitive Market

The fashion market has been always very competitive right from the beginning. There are many giant organization dominating in the market. The market has been occupied by the company like Zara, H&M, Uniqulo, TopShop and such. There are the company with least weaknesses and has overcome the threats and they are the market leaders. This is a huge threats for the Forever 21 to share the same market place within the same industry (Lutz, 2013).

6

3.4.2 Fake Imitations

There are many dishonest organizations those do not have their own design and they try to imitate the design as well as pattern of the Forever 21. Those organizations are doing the imitation illegally and that is a biggest threats for the Forever 21. Because they are offering the same designed products in a cheaper price (Lutz, 2013).

4. TOWS Analysis of Forever 21

One of the weaknesses that can come up with biggest threats for the Forever 21 from their competitor because of narrow customer segmentation, they only focusing on young adults when all other competitor are focusing almost every segment of customer. Also from privet organization it's almost impossible for solving all the problem and treats.

Threats that can predicting for Forever 21 fake imitating and risk from the competitor when its able for Forever 21 to defeat it with their strength, because the latest trend with affordable price it's not that easy for competitor take over, also making fake imitation is not goanna effect because of quality and customer satisfaction is inimitable.

The opportunities for customizing cloth and for increasing demand which is leaking cause of their weaknesses like private organization is slow to making and taking decision with large change.

Strength is the factor that always brings opportunities for organization. The main strength detected in the SWOT are Latest treading product and design with affordable for their customer which is a positivity for increasing the needs of youngsters to stick to trends, also for creating needs for customize clothing's

5. Conclusion

Forever 21 is one of the biggest fashion companies in the world providing customers with many fashion trends. Therefore, they have to keep in mind of their strengths and especially weaknesses. The company faces a number of problems in and around the globe. As mentioned above in the SWOT analysis, it can be seen that how the weaknesses can strike upon the strengths and threats can be takeover by the opportunities. Hence, not only forever 21 but their branches have to think about the consequences which follow. Only by keeping them in mind, the company can go ahead and succeed in the business life. Regardless all those negative aspects overcoming the weaknesses and threats can provide Forever 21 to go smoothly and take the full advantages of the fast and advance market as well as to sustain within the industry by capitalize the revenue.

6. References

Batheja, A. R. (2018). Forever 21 Celebrates the Opening of Its All New Revamped Store at the Mall of India With an International Twist. Retrieved from Business Wire India: https://businesswireindia.com/news/fulldetails/forever-21-celebrates-opening-its-all-new-revamped-store-at-mall-india-with-international-twist/60695

Christopher, M. (2011). Logistics & Supply Management. Great Britain: PEARSON. Retrieved from http://www.icesi.edu.co/blogs/supplychain0714/files/2014/07/Martin_Christopher_Logistics_and_Supply_Chain_Management_4th_Edition____2011-1.pdf

Deloitte. (2017). Disruptions in Retail through Digital Transformation. Retrieved from https://www2.deloitte.com/content/dam/Deloitte/in/Documents/CIP/in-cip-disruptions-in-retail-noexp.pdf

Forbes.com. (2018). America's Largest Private Companies 2018. Retrieved from Forbes; #123 Forever 21: https://www.forbes.com/companies/forever-21/#d50c98e365fd

FOREVER 21 Official Website. (2018). ABOUT US. Retrieved from FOREVER 21 Official Website : https://www.forever21.com/eu/shop/info/aboutus

Gomes, R. C. (2006). Stakeholder Management in the Local Government Decision-Making Area: Evidences from a Triangulation Study with the English Local Government. Retrieved from http://www.scielo.br/pdf/bar/v3n1/v3n1a05.pdf

GÜREL, E. (2017). SWOT ANALYSIS: A THEORETICAL REVIEW. The Journal of International Social Research, 996. Retrieved from http://www.sosyalarastirmalar.com/cilt10/sayi51_pdf/6iksisat_kamu_isletme/gurel_emet.pdf

GÜREL, E. (2017). SWOT ANALYSIS: A THEORETICAL REVIEW. The Journal of International Social Research. doi:http://dx.doi.org/10.17719/jisr.2017.1832

GÜREL, E. (2017). SWOT ANALYSIS: A THEORETICAL REVIEW. The Journal of International Social Research, 10, 996. doi:http://dx.doi.org/10.17719/jisr.2017.1832

GÜREL, E. (2018). SWOT ANALYSIS: A THEORETICAL REVIEW. The Journal of International Social Research. doi:10.17719/jisr.2017.1832

Lutz, A. (2013). Why Forever 21 Is Crushing Everyone Else In The Teen Retail Industry. Retrieved from BusinessInsider: https://www.businessinsider.com/why-forever-21-is-winning-teen-retail-2013-11/?IR=T

MARSH, A. (2018). Forever 21's Pre-Black Friday 2018 Sale Will Help Get Your Wardrobe To Peak Hygge. Retrieved from Elite Daily: https://www.elitedaily.com/p/forever-21s-pre-black-friday-2018-sale-will-help-get-your-wardrobe-to-peak-hygge-13173670

MartinRoll. (2018). Forever 21 – Fast Fashion Retail Brand With An Edge. Retrieved from MartinRoll: Business & Brand Leadership: https://martinroll.com/resources/articles/branding/forever21-fast-fashion-with-an-edge/

Montes, S. (2018). This Forever 21 x The Grinch Collection Will Make Your Heart Grow 3 Sizes This Year. Retrieved from Elite Daily: https://www.elitedaily.com/p/this-forever-21-x-the-grinch-collection-will-make-your-heart-grow-3-sizes-this-year-13119728

Persad, M. (2015). 8 Times Forever21 Looked Anything But Cheap. Retrieved from Huffpost: https://www.huffpost.com/entry/forever21-anything-but-cheap_n_56266d95e4b02f6a900df7ac

Wiseman, E. (2011). The gospel according to Forever 21. Retrieved from The Guairdian : https://www.theguardian.com/lifeandstyle/2011/jul/17/forever-21-fast-fashion-america

YOUR KNOWLEDGE HAS VALUE

- We will publish your bachelor's and
  master's thesis, essays and papers

- Your own eBook and book -
  sold worldwide in all relevant shops

- Earn money with each sale

Upload your text at www.GRIN.com
and publish for free